the little book of
MEDITATIONS

gilly pickup

summersdale

THE LITTLE BOOK OF MEDITATIONS

Summersdale Publishers Ltd
46 West Street
Chichester
West Sussex
PO19 1RP
UK

www.summersdale.com

Printed and bound in the Czech Republic

ISBN: 978-1-84953-864-0

Substantial discounts on bulk quantities of Summersdale books are available to corporations, professional associations and other organisations. For details contact general enquiries: telephone: +44 (0) 1243 771107, fax: +44 (0) 1243 786300 or email: enquiries@summersdale.com.

INTRODUCTION

When daily pressures threaten to engulf you, look to the inner sanctum of your mind. We all need quiet time to recharge our batteries and meditation is the perfect way to achieve that peace. If you practise on a regular basis, you could discover that meditation is the most effective, stress-busting technique there is. Better still, it is free, can be done in your own home, needs no specialist equipment and is scientifically approved.

The greatest prayer
is patience.

Buddha

A calm mind is not
disturbed by the
waves of thoughts.

Remez Sasson

WHAT IS MEDITATION?

Meditation is a process of awareness leading to a state of consciousness which brings serenity and clarity. During meditation sessions the body is in a state of rest and relaxation. When you meditate you are fully awake and alert, but your mind is not focused on the external world or on events taking place around you. The goal is to achieve inner peace.

The important thing is not to stop questioning. Curiosity has its own reason for existing.

Albert Einstein

MEDITATION IS A TECHNIQUE FOR RESTING THE MIND

The word meditation comes from the Latin words *meditari* – to think, to dwell upon, to exercise the mind – and *mederi* – to heal. The Sanskrit word *medha* means wisdom. When practised, meditation enables you to reach a state of consciousness which is totally different from the normal waking state. The goal is not to get rid of thoughts but to become more aware of the 'silence' that is present in the mind along with the thoughts. It is the means for experiencing the centre of consciousness within ourselves. When we cultivate a peaceful mind, it follows that we feel good and positive within. Meditation brings mental, emotional and spiritual balance, which is the key to enlightenment.

The gift of learning
to **meditate** is the
greatest **gift** you
can give yourself in
this **lifetime**.

Sogyal Rinpoche

The best way to meditate is through meditation itself.

Ramana Maharshi

MEDITATION BRINGS MANY BENEFITS

Besides reducing stress and relieving muscle tension, meditation can help us make better decisions, which leads to higher productivity at work. It increases creativity and mental alertness and may aid problem-solving, too, making meditation an excellent means of improving physical and emotional well-being. Some find the best time to meditate is in the evening, at the end of their working day; if practised at that time, it has the extra bonus of helping ensure a deep, peaceful sleep. Whatever time we choose, the act of meditating provides us with an oasis of calm that is often hard to find in our busy lives. If you or someone you know suffers from a mental illness, meditation should only be used under expert guidance. Should you have any doubts about your personal or mental health, see a medical practitioner.

Meditation can
help us embrace
our worries, our fear,
our anger; and that
is very healing.

Thích Nhất Hạnh

Every experience, no matter how bad it seems, holds with it a blessing of some kind. The goal is to find it.

Buddha

ANYONE CAN LEARN TO MEDITATE

The good news is it doesn't matter who you are, how old you are, what gender you are or what your nationality is, because meditation is for everyone. You don't need to be religious, or to have a guru, and you don't have to spend lots of time in an ashram to learn the art. Meditation requires little to no equipment or physical exertion and so can be a good fit for those with a time- or cash-strapped lifestyle. Meditation, like exercise, can trigger a release of endorphins, the brain chemical that makes you feel good. Granted, some people find it easier than others, and some take longer to 'get the hang of it' because like any skill, meditation requires practice to achieve satisfying results. However, anyone at all can do it and, with perseverance, will reap the benefits.

YOU CAN SIT IN A VARIETY OF POSITIONS WHEN MEDITATING

Most people think of the lotus position when they think of meditating; sitting cross-legged and placing each leg on top of the thigh opposite. Although famous, the lotus is not necessary in practice. It is difficult for some people to master and indeed, even with practice, some may never manage it. If you don't want to – or can't – meditate while in this position, then simply find a peaceful place to sit in a chair with your back straight and eyes closed. It is important to choose a position that is comfortable for you and that you can maintain throughout your meditation session. If you use a chair, pick one with a flat seat so that you don't find yourself tilting too much towards the back. If your feet don't touch the floor, find something for them to rest on so that your legs don't dangle.

WITHIN YOURSELF IS A STILLNESS, A SANCTUARY TO WHICH YOU CAN RETREAT AT ANY TIME AND BE YOURSELF.

Hermann Hesse

At the end of the day, I can end up just totally wacky, because I've made mountains out of molehills. With meditation, I can keep them as molehills.

Ringo Starr

FIND AN UNCLUTTERED, TRANQUIL PLACE TO MEDITATE

It should be somewhere you will not be disturbed. Bring your awareness through all parts of your body and allow your muscles to relax, except those supporting your head, neck and back. Revel in and enjoy the calming process of letting go of your body tension. Meditation is the science of letting go and this begins with the body and then extends to your thoughts.

Meditation allows us to
directly participate in
our lives instead of living
life as an afterthought.

Stephen Levine

MEDITATION IS A POWERFUL HABIT

Besides being powerful, meditation is also an extremely simple practice and, better still, it brings immediate benefits. Some people think of meditation as something you do with a teacher, and of course, some people prefer to attend meditation classes, but it can be as simple as paying attention to your breathing while sitting in your car, at your desk, on a bus, doing some form of exercise or while out walking. Qigong or t'ai chi are examples of meditating while in motion. We explore these later in the book. You can practise meditation wherever you happen to be. While forming the habit can be a little frustrating, try to overcome the initial feeling of obligation when considering your meditation routine and anticipate the benefits instead. Remember, a little meditation each day helps to keep stress and negativity away.

The secret of **change** is to focus all of your **energy**, not on fighting the old, but on building the **new**.

Socrates

The thing about
meditation is…
you become more
and more you.

David Lynch

WHEN MEDITATING, TRY TO KEEP YOUR MIND FREE FROM UNWANTED THOUGHTS

It can be very difficult for a beginner to the art of meditation to sit still for any length of time and think of nothing or have an empty mind. Trying to do that often simply encourages more random thoughts to flit through our minds. In general, the easiest way to begin meditating is by focusing on breathing to help concentration and let it develop from there. If your room is artificially lit, perhaps use the dimmer switch to create low lighting, or sit by candlelight. It helps the feeling of relaxation. Tilt the head slightly downward, with eyes open or closed. Tilting your head helps open up the chest and eases your breathing. End your session by sitting quietly for a moment or two and gently stretching your arms and legs before getting up.

Meditation stops the sound-loving **mind.**

Sri Chinmoy

Half an hour's
meditation each day is
essential, except when
you are busy. Then a
full hour is needed.

Saint Francis de Sales

BECOME ONE WITH YOURSELF

With your hands resting in your lap or on your knees, turn your mind inwards, making a mental note about which parts of your body feel most relaxed. Sometimes, your body can tense in reaction to your intense, inward focus. Although this may sound contradictory, focus on relaxing. Release any muscles that are tensed but not supporting you. Become aware of any subtle movements of your body, such as grinding your teeth or clenching your hands, and let your body fall into stillness. Now turn your awareness to your mood, becoming aware of what it is like without judgement. Next, remind yourself that there is nothing for you to 'do' while you are here; just sit and let everything unfold. It all becomes simpler the more often you practise.

THERE IS NO 'RIGHT' AND 'WRONG' WAY TO MEDITATE

When you start meditating, do not expect it to 'work' for you straight away. It is easy to blame yourself but it could be that you need more time or the method you are using isn't suitable for you.

If you find it very hard to get into 'meditation mode' and after a few sessions feel you are getting nowhere, it may help to start to practise different meditation techniques, including those explored in this book. You never know what will work for you, even something completely unexpected such as standing on your head! It's unconventional, true, but as long as it works and you are enjoying all the benefits of meditation, stand on your head all you like!

Let it come, let it go,
let it flow.

Khenpo Tsewang Dongyal Rinpoche

MEDITATION IS LISTENING TO THE DIVINE WITHIN.

Edgar Cayce

THERE ARE MANY DIFFERENT MEDITATION TECHNIQUES TO CHOOSE FROM

Some people may concentrate on breathing, consciously noticing the movement of air in and out of the nostrils. Alternatively, there are grounding and mindfulness practices, which entail simply being aware of sensations, feelings and thoughts, observing them without passing judgement. Perhaps you could try 'focused attention meditation', if you prefer to keep your mind and attention on something. Choose an external object as the subject of your prolonged attention. Others may choose to empty their mind by gently pushing aside any straggling thoughts or by allowing thoughts to float in and out of their awareness.

BUDDHIST MEDITATIONS

Buddhist meditation covers various meditation practices which aim to develop mindfulness, concentration, tranquillity and insight.

The Mindfulness of Breathing meditation, a basic breath-counting technique, is, as the name suggests, based on being mindful or having an increased awareness of yourself, your actions and experiences. The exercise is simple: while meditating count to ten repeatedly, focusing on your breath. Every time you are distracted by a thought, acknowledge it calmly and begin counting again.

Shikantaza, or 'just sitting', doesn't utilise focus on any particular object but instead the practitioner should simply try to stay as in the moment as possible, observing their thoughts and surroundings.

ACTIVE MEDITATIONS: QIGONG, YOGA AND T'AI CHI

Qigong, a traditional Chinese practice, combines meditation, relaxation and breathing exercises to restore and maintain balance. It is designed to raise self-awareness and balance life energy by exploring the connection between body, mind and spirit. Yoga is a series of postures and controlled breathing exercises performed to promote a more flexible body and calm mind. Moving through poses encourages you to focus less on distracting thoughts and more on the moment. T'ai chi, sometimes referred to as 'meditation in motion', is a form of gentle Chinese martial arts which combines deep breathing and relaxation with slow and gentle movements. Originally developed in thirteenth-century China, it is practised today worldwide. The deliberate, controlled movements and intense concentration required help still the mind and give a deeper sense of relaxation.

A **free** and silent
mind is always in
meditation.

Remez Sasson

An Awakened person
is someone who finds
freedom in good
fortune and bad.

Bodhidharma

LOTS OF THINGS CAN BE MEDITATION

Whether you are being aware of your breathing, relaxing by the side of a lake, listening to the birds sing, or simply chilling and doing nothing in particular, it is meditation. If these and similar activities are free from distractions, it is effective meditation. Meditation is essentially focused attention, which when practised daily helps us to draw on its benefits when needed.

If we could see the
miracle of a single
flower clearly, our whole
life would change.

Buddha

FOCUS ENABLES YOU TO DISPEL YOUR MIND'S JUMBLED THOUGHTS

Meditation has been practised for thousands of years and was originally meant to result in an understanding of life's sacred forces. Done regularly, meditation produces a deep state of relaxation and encourages the mind to become more peaceful. During meditation, you eliminate the flow of muddled thoughts that in daily life can crowd your mind and cause stress. As you proceed and continue your meditation sessions, you will see the beneficial effect it has on your mental clarity, instilling a feeling of peace in your daily life. Issues which are thorny or confusing will potentially become more manageable using the tool kit of meditation: a higher awareness of your thoughts means you are better equipped to filter out emotional or irrational responses.

Knowing yourself
is the beginning
of all wisdom.

Aristotle

Life is a mystery –
mystery of **beauty**,
bliss and divinity.
Meditation is the **art** of
unfolding that mystery.

Amit Ray

TAKE TIME TO MEDITATE

Try to allow a minimum of 15 minutes for meditation each day. Depending on day-to-day matters and personal issues, it can take up to ten minutes or even longer for the mind to become calm. Be prepared to set aside a little extra time for your session, so you don't feel as though you're watching the clock. In each practice session, your body benefits from a state of deep rest and relaxation.

Meditate daily, and soon
your inner strength and
mind power will grow.

Remez Sasson

MEDITATION HELPS US ACHIEVE AN INNER PEACE AND THE CAPACITY TO RESPOND TO SITUATIONS CALMLY

After your first meditation practice you may feel calmer and more focused. When you start to meditate on a regular basis, you start to develop the ability to bring these feelings into practice in everyday life, to study a situation objectively and consciously choose how you want to respond. The gift of being present and aware is invaluable in dealing with others. Meditation is a fantastic tool for bringing harmony into our relationships and, with regular practice, your ability to harness feelings of calm and be less reactive to stressful situations will keep on improving.

RELAX WHILE YOU MEDITATE

Sometimes, particularly with beginners to the art, trying to meditate can be akin to trying to fall asleep; the harder we try the more impossible it seems. One way around this is to think of meditation as a welcome opportunity to relax rather than as a discipline you have to master. If your attention wanders, try to practise acceptance and avoid getting annoyed with yourself. Simply direct your attention back to what you are doing and focus on your experience at that moment.

It helps to wear comfortable clothes when you are meditating. Avoid wearing anything too tight or material that may be uncomfortable. It is best to wear loose clothing, such as sportswear or nightwear.

Meditation is the golden key to all the mysteries of life.

Bhagwan Shree Rajneesh

IF YOU ARE DOING
MINDFULNESS
MEDITATION,
YOU ARE DOING
IT WITH YOUR
ABILITY TO ATTEND
TO THE MOMENT.

Daniel Goleman

UNLEASH THE POWER OF YOUR MIND TO MAXIMISE HEALTH, HAPPINESS AND WELL-BEING

People can feel themselves becoming stressed in response to a multitude of daily events, from missing a bus or forgetting a birthday to feeling they are not up to the task in hand. Although we are consciously aware that these are not life-or-death situations, the body experiences the amount of stress as excessive and so triggers the 'fight or flight' mechanism. This diverts bodily resources away from systems such as the digestive or immune systems and towards the body's muscular and emotional needs. This constant deprivation can have physical side effects such as a frail immune system. Meditation eases stress and when practised regularly will enable you to feel increasingly less anxious during potentially triggering situations, improving your emotional and physical health.

REASONS FOR MEDITATING

Meditation is a simple, fast way to reduce stress. During most of our waking life our minds are engaged in a continuous internal dialogue in which the meaning and emotional associations of one thought triggers the next. Meditation helps calm the inner turmoil, getting rid of the chatter in our minds. It can also help alleviate anxiety, high blood pressure, insomnia and chronic pain, decrease muscle tension and improve mental performance.

Meditate, visualise
and create your
own reality and the
universe will simply
reflect back to you.

Amit Ray

Be still and know.

Aristotle

BE AWARE OF HOW YOU BREATHE

If you are new to meditation, you may find your attention drifting away from your breathing. Don't be discouraged. As soon as you realise this is happening, gently focus on bringing it back. It doesn't matter if this happens several times during your practice sessions. As you begin to master the art, you will find it becomes easier to concentrate.

If you want to
conquer the
anxiety of life,
live in the **moment**,
live in the **breath**.

Amit Ray

Meditation helps
me deal with life's
ups and downs.

Eva Mendes

MEDITATION IS NOT ABOUT OPTING OUT OF LIFE OR STOPPING OUR THOUGHTS

The aim of meditation is not to achieve a totally blank mind, devoid of all thoughts. It teaches us to clear our minds of unwanted worries and just 'be' in the present moment. This means we are not distracted by unwanted thoughts but are able to turn a more intense attention to whatever it is we want to consider – almost the opposite of a blank mind! Similarly, utilising meditation because you don't want to think any more, perhaps because your worries are too great, will not be successful. In those instances, perhaps consider other therapies alongside a course of meditation. Meditation can complement talking therapies and CBT (cognitive behavioural therapy). However, always ask your therapist for their recommendation before introducing it into your mental health treatment.

CONSIDER WHAT YOU WANT MEDITATION TO DO FOR YOU

People meditate for a multitude of reasons. Some do it to help them to visualise a goal they want to achieve, while some meditate to quiet their inner turmoil. Others do it to improve their creativity – a tumultuous mind does not always mean a brain crowded with negative thoughts; sometimes it's one that is simply overstuffed with ideas. Meditation allows you to forge a path through the ideas and focus on just one project. Meditation

The most weighty truths may strike, but without meditation cannot enter and influence the mind.

John Thornton

WHEN QUESTIONS ARISE, STAY FOCUSED AND MINDFUL

If you are a beginner in the art of meditating, it is natural to question what you are doing and perhaps why you feel it is not working as you expected. Maybe you simply feel like giving up, or you may even think that you are wasting your time. Be kind to yourself and remember that meditation is a skill to be learnt, and as with all skills this takes time. Stay focused on your goal and persist. You wouldn't expect yourself to be instantly good at basketball within weeks of starting to learn to play, or fluent at German as soon as you take your first lesson. Know that doubts naturally arise in the process of learning, and consider them 'risings of the mind', to be observed and then discarded.

Meditation is the **tongue** of the **soul** and the **language** of our spirit.

Jeremy Taylor

We tend to think of
meditation in only
one way. But life itself
is a meditation.

Raúl Juliá

MEDITATION MEANS GIVING YOUR UNDIVIDED ATTENTION

When concentrating, thoughts will probably come into your mind about unrelated subjects, or you may even ask yourself, 'Am I doing this properly?' It is not the thought that disturbs you, but your reaction to it. Every thought will seem to require some response, whether it's an interest in taking the thought further or an effort to get rid of it. However, if you acknowledge the thought when it enters your mind and then simply let it go, you will remain focused. Unfortunately this also means you can't meditate with one half of your brain while the other composes a work email or shopping list. One of the issues with modern life is the drive to fit so much stuff in that you are constantly multitasking. Allow yourself the luxury of your own undivided attention.

LIFE IS REALLY SIMPLE, BUT WE INSIST ON MAKING IT COMPLICATED.

Confucius

Meditation has
to become your
heartbeat; even when
you are asleep the
meditation continues
like an undercurrent.

Bhagwan Shree Rajneesh

MEDITATE MORE THAN ONCE A DAY

Try not to regard meditating as something you do as a 15-minute-a-day chore. Aim to imbue your whole day with the positive qualities that will develop from regular sessions. Some meditation teachers suggest a daily session of around 15 minutes as well as two, three or more shorter meditation sessions of around one or two minutes spread out over your day to revitalise your mind.

Through meditation,
the Higher Self
is experienced.

The Bhagavad Gita

MEDITATION HAS POSITIVE EFFECTS ON OUR RELATIONSHIPS

When we feel balanced and calm, it is easier to respond to stresses rationally rather than react hastily or say something we regret. Impulsive or emotion-driven reactions can create harm or upset in our relationships. While your emotions are valid, words and actions can sometimes be hasty and it is hard to be both angry and considerate. Meditation trains you to be fully present with others, helping you listen to what they are saying and have a deeper understanding of what they may actually need or desire. Your responses will be less about the 'I' and more focused on the 'us' of problem-solving within relationships.

MEDITATION HELPS US GAIN UNDERSTANDING OF OUR THOUGHTS AND PROBLEMS

Meditation allows us to observe ourselves more clearly, which in turn enables us to identify when and why we are thinking and feeling certain things. By observing our thoughts and reactions we begin to notice habits that we may have previously been unaware of. This allows us to make positive changes, and instead of being preoccupied with thoughts which dwell on the past and the future, we begin to live more in the present. After all, it is *now* that life is happening, and this is where we can make changes. In your next meditation, gently watch your thoughts and see if you can identify any pattern of thinking. You might like to mentally name them: 'worrying about the meeting next week' or 'regretting my decision'. This practice of naming may shed light on what is running through your mind.

Mindful meditation
has been discovered
to foster the ability to
inhibit those very quick
emotional impulses.

Daniel Goleman

Plant the **seed** of meditation and reap the **fruit** of peace of mind.

Remez Sasson

INCLUDE SOME MINI MEDITATIONS IN YOUR DAILY PRACTICE SESSIONS

Besides your daily meditation session of 15 or 20 minutes, try to set aside one or two shorter periods of time in the week for mini meditations. This makes sense because the more you practise meditation, the easier it becomes and the more you will see changes for the better. You may say that you have no spare time to allow more periods of meditation into your life, but if you scrutinise your daily habits you may be surprised. If you have the time to watch any old television show, fiddle with your phone or make a cup of coffee, you have spare moments which can be repurposed for meditation. All you need for your mini meditations are a couple of minutes. Start the process and start to establish the habit. Once you begin to see the benefits, you may want to spend longer doing it. The likelihood is that you will in fact get more done than you did before you started meditating.

Whenever anyone
has offended me, I try
to raise my soul so
high that the offence
cannot reach it.

René Descartes

There is nothing more
destructive than anger.

Geshe Kelsang Gyatso

DON'T THINK OF 'GOOD' AND 'BAD' MEDITATION SESSIONS

No meditation is ever 'wrong'. Some days when you finish your session you will feel more positive than you do at other times. Don't think because you are not so enthusiastic on a particular day that your meditation session 'won't work'. One individual session isn't as important as the long-term practice, so be assured that beneficial changes will certainly happen over a period of time. One tip is always to remember to be gentle with yourself;

never judgmental or harsh. It's also important to remember that it's normal for your mind to wander and it doesn't matter how many times it does this. If your meditation is the continual process of bringing your mind to the present, that is fine.

Put your heart, mind, intellect and soul even to your smallest acts. This is the secret of success.

Sivānanda Saraswati

THE GATEWAY THROUGH WHICH WE ENTER THE PATH TO ENLIGHTENMENT IS COMPASSION FOR ALL LIVING BEINGS.

Geshe Kelsang Gyatso

MEDITATION IS A REALISTIC MEANS OF CALMING YOURSELF

It teaches you how to explore your inner dimensions, to commit to yourself and, with repeated practice, lets you reach the goal of knowing yourself. Knowing yourself leads to learning about why you react to certain situations and helps you learn to react differently in the future. Meditation also helps physically: when the heart, breathing and pulse rate slows down as they do during meditation sessions, we automatically feel more tranquil.

Meditate. Live purely.
Be quiet. Do your work
with mastery. Like the
moon, come out from
behind the clouds. Shine.

Buddha

AN INTRODUCTION TO MANTRAS

Most devotees of meditation are familiar with the word 'om', meaning 'it will be' or 'to become', often used as a mantra during meditative and spiritual activities including yoga. What does 'mantra' mean? Well, the word derives from two Sanskrit words: *man*, meaning 'mind', and *tra*, which means 'instrument'. Most mantras are sacred sounds with specific, positive meanings that you repeat to yourself to uplift you and help you focus. They work on a subconscious level to calm the mind and on a conscious level they nurture the spirit with their positive affirmation. Recite your mantra with purpose and feeling. Chanting a mantra is a powerful way to enter meditation.

THERE ARE VARIOUS WAYS TO HELP STILL YOUR MIND

One effective method is to focus your attention on an object, concentrating on the shape and texture in order to block out other distractions. You might like to focus on the flame of a candle or a vase of fresh flowers for example. Gaze softly at your chosen object with your eyes fully open or partially closed, creating a gentle, diffused gaze. Another method is to employ movement techniques, such as yoga, qigong or t'ai chi. These exercises still your mind by coordinating your breath and body with gentle movement. Some prefer to use mantra meditation – where a calming word or phrase is repeated over and over, either aloud or silently and sometimes timed with the breath, to focus the attention and prevent distracting thoughts from disrupting your meditation.

Meditation... is
bringing the mind
home to our true **self.**

Sogyal Rinpoche

Meditation is not the menu; it's the meal.

Victor Davich

MANTRAS HELP FOCUS YOU DURING MEDITATION SESSIONS

Om is not the only mantra that you could use to aid your meditation. There are others, with different meanings, that you may prefer. *Lokah Samastah Sukhino Bhavantu* means, roughly, may all beings be free and happy and may I (the meditator) contribute to that happiness. This is an uplifting mantra celebrating the world and your place in it. With *Om Gum Ganapatayei Namah* you bow to Ganesh, god of wisdom and destroyer of obstacles, and ask for his blessings. This could be used if you are struggling with a challenge or looking for answers. Experiment with mantras to find one that resonates with you. Other examples include *Ham-sah* or 'I am that' and *Om Namoh Shivoya* or 'I honour the divinity within myself'.

LEARN TO CULTIVATE SILENCE

We have all experienced the endless chatter that goes on in our minds. Often our thoughts seem urgent; we focus on our troubles, planning appointments or meals, or anticipating a conversation that we may have to have later. We trick ourselves into thinking this is 'productive' noise. While these thoughts can be useful sometimes, the constant 'silent noise' in our heads prevents us from embracing peace and mental quiet. Meditation is an excellent way to calm the relentless chatter and enable us to have some mental clarity, peace and quiet, putting aside the rest of our life for a moment and focusing on our own health.

The **quieter** you become, the more you can **hear.**

Ram Dass

When you meditate,
the silence of the senses
illumines the presence
of God within.

Gurumayi Chidvilasananda

MEDITATE ONLY WHEN FULLY AWAKE

You need to be wide awake when you attempt to meditate, otherwise it becomes very easy to doze off. If you feel tired, it makes sense to wait until you feel more alert. Even though it sounds counterintuitive, it is fine and even in places encouraged to meditate after a cup of coffee. Or perhaps you need to wait until a particular time in the day, when your energy levels are at their greatest.

Meditation is the
dissolution of thoughts
in eternal awareness or
pure consciousness.

Sivānanda Saraswati

TRY MEDITATION AT WORK

Work is one of the biggest sources of stress in our lives, and making important decisions in the workplace is a reality for many of us. Ideally, we are our best, professional selves when doing so, but we are also only human. We may clash with colleagues or feel the pressure of a particularly impactful dilemma. Using a mini meditation or even a normal-length one at work can really help to calm the mind and focus our faculties. Without the cloud of emotion covering the correct path, we are able to take logical and effective actions. You can meditate whilst walking to your next meeting as a form of movement technique. You can even meditate whilst carrying out gentle, repetitive tasks that don't require more than a handful of actions, such as photocopying documents. Avoid meditating during any task that requires mental attention as it will not benefit your meditation session and certainly won't benefit your work!

OUR MINDS ARE BY NATURE PEACEFUL

If you consider the factors that are playing out across your mind, you may be surprised by how many are introduced by societal pressures or 'manufactured' worries. While it's natural to be concerned about the 'essentials' in life, such as safe living conditions or mental and physical health, worries such as what other people may think of you are generated by societal pressures. We often look for things that we can be negative and concerned about when really we would be much healthier and happier if we let a lot of our worries go. Meditation is a helpful tool to relax us, calm us down and make us more appreciative of life's pleasures. It is a shame that we often allow stress and fatigue to obscure the beauty there is all around us; when we are calm and centred, it is much easier to appreciate all that is good in life.

You must find the place
inside yourself where
nothing is impossible.

Deepak Chopra

QUIET THE MIND AND THE SOUL WILL SPEAK.

Ma Jaya Sati Bhagavati

CONSIDER GUIDED MEDITATION

Guided meditation is where a teacher or guide works you through a meditation, helping you to form mental images of situations or places that you find help to take you into a state of relaxation. This is achieved by using all your senses – sounds, smells, sights, touch and sometimes even taste. Some guided meditations have a specific purpose, such as healing, improving relationships or bringing prosperity and abundance into your life. Other guided meditations are more general and aim to quiet the mind and soothe the soul. Even those with a regular meditation practice can benefit from being taken through guided meditation by a qualified teacher.

FEEL LIGHTER AND HAPPIER

Repeated practice of meditation can not only help with difficult situations and bad moods but also improve your outlook on life as a whole, making you feel more positive, confident and relaxed. It is logical that when your life is less burdened by worry and stress, you then have the mental space to consider what makes it enjoyable. With your improved ability to handle stressful situations, little frustrations such as late trains or missed deliveries are less likely to have a negative impact on your mood, and you are more able to notice the wonder in your environment such as, for example, a beautiful sunset or the feel of fresh air on your face. When you feel more positive on the inside, you will notice more positivity in your everyday life.

Remember that wherever your heart is, there you will find your treasure.

Paulo Coelho

Meditation is not a
means to an end. It
is both the means
and the end.

Jiddu Krishnamurti

BEING TRULY PRESENT IN EACH MOMENT IS WHEN WE EXTRACT THE GREATEST MEANING FROM OUR LIVES

Nowadays there is often so much going on around us that it becomes impossible to call a halt to the thoughts, feelings and anxieties churning around our brains. Often we focus on those feelings rather than our experiences and the environment around us. Meditation helps us live in the moment and become fully aware of our choices, actions and experiences.

We should not live only a tiny fraction of our inner selves; we should savour the whole of life. Meditation helps us to do just that.

MEDITATION HELPS DEVELOP YOUR CREATIVE SKILLS

Consider that we all have many thousands of thoughts each day, every day. The trouble is, many of these thoughts are the same ones popping up unbidden every day. We churn them round our mind, obsessively, again and again. This means there is no space for new thoughts or new and inspirational ideas. Meditation is a powerful practice for going beyond conditioned thought patterns, leading us into a state of expanded awareness and allowing us to open up to new ideas. Meditation creates the mental and emotional conditions in which creativity is most likely to grow.

Words are but the **shell**; meditation is the **kernel**.

Bahya ibn Paquda

Your mind is a powerful thing. When you filter it with positive thoughts, your life will start to change.

Buddha

TAKE TIME TO SIT STILL AND REFLECT

Nowadays we are all so busy that at times we feel there is simply no opportunity to sit still and reflect – that it is time wasted. Successful meditation needs your inner self to be still so that the mind becomes silent. When that happens and you have no distractions your meditative state deepens, and tension dissolves. So the time you spend meditating, far from encroaching on your busy day, can be the most beneficial part of it. In fact, the time when you are most busy and stressed is when you need to meditate the most! Giving your mind time off from the pressures of daily life gets you back in touch with your inner self. It can connect you to your inner knowing and help you find the answers you have been searching for within yourself. What could be better than that?

Your **goal** is not to battle with the mind, but to **witness** the mind.

Muktananda

Silence is the sleep that
nourishes wisdom.

Francis Bacon

KEEP A MEDITATION DIARY

Some of those who practice meditation like to record their experiences. It can be helpful to the process, particularly for those new to the art, because it lets you see in black and white what you experienced, and how you felt during and after. With the benefit of hindsight you can then analyse the session and see what was different that made an impact. It aids in highlighting any distractions that occur during your sessions, so can ensure you are practising at the best time in the best environment. A journal can also be a great motivation tool. You will be able to see how your struggles and negative thinking diminish over time and how your mind changes as your practice deepens.

MEDITATION IS NOT A PART OF ANY RELIGION

Meditation is to be found in every major spiritual tradition – not just Eastern religions such as Buddhism but those emanating from the Middle and Near East such as Islam and Christianity. But there is no need for those who meditate to be religious or to follow any particular religion to benefit from the practice. It has nothing to do with beliefs or doctrines but is a straightforward mental technique that can help us reach the inner sanctum of our minds. However, if you so wish, once you have learned basic meditation skills, you can expand your meditation practice to explore more spiritual aspects, such as visualising a light or an embodiment of your god. Yoga, prayer and contemplation can also help you tap into your spiritual side. Choose what works for you: there are no hard and fast rules. Do whatever you enjoy!

MEDITATION IS A FLOWER AND COMPASSION IS ITS FRAGRANCE.

Bhagwan Shree Rajneesh

That which we
do not bring to
consciousness appears
in our lives as fate.

Carl Jung

DISPLAY YOUR FAVOURITE MEDITATION QUOTES

Choose those nuggets of wisdom which resonate most with you. Pin them on a wall by your desk, on the refrigerator, in the bathroom, somewhere prominent so that it is easy for you to look at them several times every day. The more often you read them the more effective they become until eventually they will seem like second nature.

Meditation and concentration are the way to a life of serenity.

Remez Sasson

TAKE IT EASY AFTER YOU FINISH A MEDITATION SESSION

When you finish a meditation session, don't just jump up and start the next activity. Consider what you are going to do next – make a cup of coffee, take the dog for a walk, make your way to the bus stop and catch the bus to work – whatever it happens to be. Hold on to that feeling of calm you created during your meditation; keep it close and take it with you to your next task. Remind yourself throughout the day of the feeling that the focused attention of the meditation gave you. Take some deep breaths and recall your meditation session, and then notice how that makes you feel. By doing this repeatedly, the qualities that you cultivate in your meditation practice will naturally carry over into your daily life.

The more man
meditates upon good
thoughts, the **better**
will be his world and
the **world** at large.

Confucius

When meditation is
mastered, the mind is
unwavering like the
flame of a candle in
a windless place.

The Bhagavad Gita

THE ART OF MEDITATING LEADS TO FULFILMENT

Can you say that you truly feel fulfilled? If you have to stop and think about it, then you probably don't. Are you one of those people who races round frantically, trying to get everything done and dusted in time for a deadline? If you are, then stop! Now that you have read through most of this book, you know you have an ally in the art of meditation. Go to your private space, your 'meditation corner', and take 15 or 20 minutes to clear the churning in your head, to focus your busy mind. Let go of daily concerns and allow meditation to bring you the serenity you deserve. A regular meditation practice will help you feel calm and centred. By spending some quiet time with yourself, you will soothe your mind and create space for happiness and contentment to take hold.

Spend some **time alone** every day.

Dalai Lama

Meditation helps concentration of the mind. Then the mind is free from thoughts and is in the meditated form.

Ramana Maharshi

SO YOU'VE READ THIS BOOK AND STILL AREN'T SURE IF MEDITATION IS FOR YOU

If you need more convincing, then here are some benefits in a nutshell as to why it makes sense to start meditating on a daily basis. Roll those credits for the following reasons, including: it heightens your intuition, improves your memory, gives you peace of mind, teaches you to forgive, helps you make faster decisions and accomplish more, helps you enjoy better sleep, reduces your blood pressure, gives you increased energy, grants you a richer life experience, improves your listening skills, helps cultivate compassion, enhances your connection with nature, gives you a more peaceful demeanour, enables you to make more conscious choices, lets you discover who you really are, improves brain function, balances mind, body and spirit, and is easier than you think!

MEDITATION AND A BALANCED LIFE

And finally, when meditating alone or without guidance, it is important to remember that these sessions are part of living a balanced life. Meditation should not be used to withdraw from life or for the avoidance of private or practical issues. Consider meditation a tool to assist you in embracing all aspects of your life and considering your place in the world. As with any new activity, above all things the practice of meditation should contribute to your happiness.

the little book of
RESILIENCE

lucy lane

ISBN: 978-1-84953-830-5

the little book of
RELAXATION

lucy lane

ISBN: 978-1-84953-787-2

the little book of
POSITIVITY

lucy lane

ISBN: 978-1-84953-788-9

the little book of
MEDITATIONS

gilly pickup

ISBN: 978-1-84953-864-0

the little book of
AFFIRMATIONS

gilly pickup

ISBN: 978-1-84953-863-3

the little book of
INSPIRATION

lucy lane

ISBN: 978-1-84953-843-5

the little book of
COMFORT

lucy lane

ISBN: 978-1-84953-793-3

the little book of
FRIENDSHIP

lucy lane

ISBN: 978-1-84953-862-6

the little book of
HAPPINESS

lucy lane

THE LITTLE BOOK OF HAPPINESS

Lucy Lane

£5.99
Hardback
ISBN: 978-1-84953-790-2

Sometimes the hurly-burly of daily life leads our happiness levels to sink a little. But don't worry! This joyful little book is packed with inspiring quotations and simple, easy-to-follow tips that will help you unwind, relax and greet life with a smile.

If you're interested in finding out
more about our books, find us on
Facebook at **Summersdale Publishers**
and follow us on Twitter at
@Summersdale.

www.summersdale.com